In Joseph Minden's roaming p(
the strange suspended present
in England. Kings and old po(
and Berlusconi, all jostle in the
between sea and land, in verse t.   ... ... now the
veil / between the worlds / is thin" when we are attending carefully
enough, when our minds have the chance to wander, disconcerted,
bored and free.

— Isabella Hammad, *Enter Ghost*

A tear-shaped slice of rock crystal enclosed in gold becomes a pointer
stick for following words and these words wind around the throat of
not only *Julian Fellowes* on a high steep promontory but many others.
These others, in Joseph Minden's *Backlogues*, are components of a
national psychic shrapnel, a demented travelogue that skewers 'the
present beyond itself by the frozen image of the past'. Tim Martin is
cut to ribbons as jobs leak out of him onto the *Most Desirable Village* by
estate agent Savills. Richard Branson's grimace is stretched to the shape
of a 30-hectare private island, *nevermind*. Minden's poetry is a strange
hammer to break into the Great House Master Suite with all but two
lilies for feelers. Pinballing in the green chair, *Welcome to the History
of Great Britain. Backlogues*' acid tenderness disinters motley histories
into psychosis jerks, mooring each with birch leaves to the strangest of
drains. We're in the foothills of the South Pennines, desert Sutherland,
the Cartmel peninsula or Birkenhead Iron Works. The collision spill
of *Backlogues* links a writ of trespassing handed by Geoffrey Howe via
the monks of Birkenhead Priory to striking men at Camel Laird in
1984. The King is a Broom and will be crowned under the Holy cans
of Holsten. Now listen to all the songs on page 34.

— Cole Denyer, *Ah, Beautiful Sky*

Joseph Minden's *Backlogues* is a fine example of using the long form
poem to provide both a diaristic entry into lockdown literature's
growing archive, and a slow, patient, colourful gradation of all the
mundane joys we hold dear in times of duress and hardship. Part late-
modernist pastoral, part epic, part autotheoretical collage, part musical
performance, it is a poem that establishes a space and time for thinking
at a pace that runs against the ways we internalise productivity and
repress desire in times of crisis.

— Azad Ashim Sharma, *Ergastulum: Vignettes of Lost Time*

BACKLOGUES

Joseph Minden is a poet and schoolteacher based in Brighton. His books *Poppy* (Carcanet) and *Paddock Calls: The Nightbook* (slub press) both came out in 2022.

Also by Joseph Minden

Poppy (Carcanet, 2022)

Paddock Calls: The Nightbook (Slub Press, 2022)

Backlogues

Joseph Minden

Broken Sleep Books

ISBN: 978-1-915760-23-4

Cover designed by Aaron Kent

Edited by James Byrne

Typeset by Aaron Kent

Broken Sleep Books Ltd
Rhydwen
Talgarreg
Ceredigion
SA44 4HB

Broken Sleep Books Ltd
Fair View
St Georges Road
Cornwall
PL26 7YH

Contents

Yet hard the task to heal the bleeding heart,
To bid the still-recurring thoughts depart;
Hush the loud grief, and stem the rising sigh,
And curb rebellious passion with reply;
Calmly to dwell on all that pleased before,
And yet to know that all can please no more.
      — *The Village*, George Crabbe

And the challenge of space in my soul
be filled by the shape I become.
        — Martin Carter

Who's that
        whistle in the distant
kitchen
                    kettle going
spray arc
            panorama whiplash
froth down scroll
            white sea-script
pulse of old
                buy habits
tea pools on the
                    sunburst
day supplied
                resolve to
more past tense
                in silence
thoughts so
        wingful black scatter
in the green
            bleached clumps
and wet teeth rattle
            at the skylights

Noup Head
                    catching the sun
far off this cloud
                    one toothpick
its dear
                    regular light
when dark
                    goes over
my maudlin boat
                    pitched in TV
yawing
                    Belgravia
of Waterloo
                    bright picture
bubo yawns but
                    get this
cat mouths
                    Julian Fellowes
will see you now
          the reef screams wave
streams foam
                    and our own day

now plumes off

                    still was

the mummy assembly

                heads I know

unreachable

           the wind in ruins

lives together

       when *I* see you again

I will hold you and

              hold you

then whistle

  come back to your senses

and the kettle and

       rounding the corner

into the kitchen

                Brian

legs noodled

       in the green chair

and says

    welcome to the history

of Great Britain

          numbnuts

I didn't want him
              with me for this
his bland
                    boiled
nobbly name
              neither Charles
nor Charty Magnum
              neither Margaret
Elizabeth
                 nor Mary
so it was
      we had to settle down
and make acquaintance
                 wide arc of the
swinging blade
                 wide arc of the
breakers
           of the silence law
prescribes itself
           the space the arc
and chord
        bring into shadow

what tenpin
                on the crown
of the hill
            the Prime Minister
wearing prerogative
                as a party hat
with misdirection
        and the Magic Circle
shuffling life
                into a wine crate
Brian at his ease
                    in shade
the beech tree
                hologram above
his head
            the mighty apples
chestnuts in his lap
        me driving the lumps
the sheep
                of my dreams
out of
                the kitchen

my heart bears
                    the impression
of my patron's face
                    who owns his face
my comfort is a glad
                    enduring debt
goes Brian after me
                    the LORD gave
back what he
                    hath taken
the exception
                    by its very nature
obvious
                    my pipe the prof of
sacred regard
                    in fact
lord of the adjacent manor
                    of Slepe
the baton
                    for destroying
mixture
                    batter or dough

for it is oven day
               in lonely house
cut off by the whole
               width of the world
with real companions
               nothing flour puff
of Brian
               Kat and Bea
with slow resistant fingers
      mixing oats and syrup
as coal powders
               in the scuttle
and wood mould settles
               pigeon-chested
in the woodlouse nest
               the house is theirs
goes Kat
               we are their guests
at which
   the grisly whistle of Brian
playing a joke
               on his pipe

first of all
                    I'm sorry that
it is a man
    or someone with a name
most often linked to men
                        in truth
Brian is
                    the front part
of a head
                    transparent
time to time
                    appears as though
he takes up space
                        humanly
always two metres off
                        too bad
from Brian
    shimmering at the table
offering a bowl of
                    blueberries
scrumpled flowers
            boar-churned water

when will my cottage
   wear its hat of loam again
goats ornament
                  the county
kingly tent
               encamp my love
and root authority
            Bavarian antiquity
in atavistic Buckingham's
                  suspenders
Brian's hero
               blowing smoke
up the diplomat's
                  butthole
doesn't matter
                  dash
gone are the halcyon days
            of the jesters
I'm team Felton
   pinned down in the hall
with the hat manifesto
            and the desolation

now how did that

        come out

of the window

        clouds at pace

our environment

        desolate of livestock

Michael

        the nextdoor farmer

driving around

        with a cow head on

potato thunderdome

        my eye crawls nearer

back over the grass

        flips on the low wall

look up

        the white wall

four woodlice

        Brian fiddling

on his pipe

        and Kat turning

postcards over

        thighs on fire

I sure wouldn't mind
          having those abs
and I'd do just about
          anything
to get it
          Jillian Michaels
raging Ironheart
          hunk of
grammar destroyer
          too fit
flapjacks coming out
          scones coming out
of there
          the backs of the good
soldier silverfish
          what hearth
what homebods
          on our backs
going teaspoons
     demerera sugar-studded
butter
          oatmeal and flour

the phone rings

                            mum

it's good to hear

                        your voice

and as we walked up

            the Rochdale canal

in that box of light

                     recalling

over water bridges

               Sarson's vinegar

ducks bathing

           in the gully mouths

thoughtless of liberty

          but in profound time

together

                 leg-held by

ancestral hands

           disguised as roots

merchant converters

          good's petty limit

fell trap-like

            again and again

o

        running around

on

          the lawn

like a jet plane

        with a face mask

giving my face a hug

      you bastard for that

warehouse margin

          I want

bows and arrows

         big enough

to quiver through

       Tim Martin's face

and skewer him

        to 40,000 jobs

we pioneers

        open the doors

to our Rochdale shop

       by a small flap

in the brain's

      commercial alleyway

Brian translucent
                    as a jellyfish
stretched across
            half the twilight
Noup Head going
            at a steady wink
Bea buzzing
            Kat running about
clapping as if
                after a mosquito
white paper towel
                milk appears
on the blue grass
            drunk of night night
we were comfortable
                with the metastasis
of our liberties

                        except
what if the bum
                    is dirty
can I touch it
                will my hand

and who needs
            the streets anyway
they can take care
            of themselves
going places
                        vacantly
forehead face
            hello Bobby
no I haven't seen
            the light for fifteen
years in fact I just
            reassembled myself
out of a tin of brittle
            insect exoskeletons
A Documentary
            History of England
and the dandruff
            of my dear dad
who was a doctor
            his bald head
dry as a
            salt flat dome

stick that in your
                    pipe Brian
no predators here
          but in the evening
the huge sad cat
                    Otis or Rita
comes down the hill
     from Jeremy's workshop
and puts its maw
          round the door jamb
the sidepost
               the rusty gate hook
and though your dress
          swings beautifully Kat
I can see you are sad
                    before space
and the stars
          happy birthday mum
seventy
                    stay inside
and if you die
                    it matters not

how strait the gate
                    and far away
liquid ranges
            the Pentland Firth
gold foil
                    and pine
tremendous waste
        the plain rain in Spain
campy sprinkle
                    lopped
prospect
        acres of white marble
thunder-down
                Infanta finery
Madrid
            where no-one's
ever been
                five woodlice
drowned in the shower
            they were at work
the woodpile
                a day drier

eyes shut and

        very fast

shot over

        the last months

in fact centuries

        devastated Caithness

desert Sutherland

        forest hologram

dad taking off

        his hat

because

        he's gone

not now but

        sometime

the monks accept

        a suicide

who killed his king

        and six weeks later

vikings in the kitchen

        outburst

of the jewellery

        of innards

vampires standing around
          like bells in the ruins
ten decapitated
                    lighthouses
swivelling their eyes
          in a bullet factory
slow spray of plainsong
     crossing the causeway
invisible baptist
                    salutations
fisherman
          Bolivian salt flats
mirror to mirror if
  on earth we meet no more
we hope to meet in heaven
     I am alone and will take
everything
          where congregations
ne'er break up
          do not advise selection
I am in the igloo with
          The Lathe of Heaven

what is it of

        these islands

crosshairs

        of the present

going back

        and back

with parents

        you

Kat

        cherished

all

  the treasure has its stain

the veil

        between the worlds

is thin and as

        you step you feel

the nearness

        of the murdered

and the drowned

        the cast out

of the kingdom

        of exclusive life

and think this

                mum

your friends

              are with you

and I am still a child

        holding your hand

when I feel safe

            Brian gurning

rolling his eyes

     smug in King Charles'

nightcap

        now they will cut off

thy father's head

          you are the police

of blubbering

           don't you know

your feelings

            are a hammer

Brian bites his tongue

    and makes a steady lisp

that's just the fire

             damp logs

Kat going over
                the whale roads
with Petrarch on a lead
                damn dog
rare swimming hound
    go out into the shallows
cleanse yourself
                and die like a whale
pierced in the side
                by love's harpoon
bejewelled
                with ruby blood
a thousand
                        thousand
bobbing memories
                the lifering rim
two silhouettes
                out howling
in the North Sea
                Alfred Jewel
and lute
        of my collection

Barcelona
                    ready-ghosted
showing wind around
          to tapas for the lucky
or the brave
      still walking burnished
out of loose
                              ends
with the just-decapitated
                    contents of
the heart's museum
                    does not
actually owe
          its pastness to time
for all our histories
                    got old
in a couple of weeks
  so closed you could almost
touch them
                    me and Bea
sinking in armchairs
                    going over

Meat Loaf
  I'd Do Anything for Love
Whitney Houston
                  Run To You
Flying Lotus
            Never Catch Me
JME
            Man Don't Care
Stormzy
           Still Disappointed
Doja Cat
               Say So
John Chibadura
            Raira Vana
Lady Gaga
            Alejandro
Prince's Super Bowl
            assumption
and the trailers for
  The Thugs of Hindostan
Sholay
            Lagaan

the coals go down
        the soot blind's drawn
three streaks
                    sleep one day
further into
                    forward clocks
a time that does not
                    mark it
waves and
                    wind still walks
across
            Eynhallow Sound
the tidal indraught
                    scarcely felt
the total
                    shift
not actually felt
                    at all
contrive to play myself
                    and lie
out
                    in

the paddock
          Brian trots forward
with goat legs
      two lilies for antennae
a fringe of bilberries
      his patented oaten reed
while I
                    meanwhile
am my sovereign
      by the pool at my crown
barely more than
                    memories
two original men
                    fish but
starve in the
                lease storehouse
superior to
      the waterfall of feudal
tenure
          horizon my skirt rim
along the shore a hem
          of harrowing plots

this is how you make
        an order of yourself
one hoof
        placed delicately
in front
          the other
thus the patio masque
        with paving slabs
and arena
         translucent
gives way
        in undulation
to jerksome movement
        jellyfish prime
with virus under
        a ham-corpse
coffin hypocaust
        such ash as
bedust the lip-line
        society
false tip-off
     gut in the banquet cell

still I am
            transfixed by Brian's
dance
    out by the stunted bush
my orchard
            puny juniper shade
soaping my hands
            in Michael's milk
and olive oil
            white and yellow
English daisy
                English egg
Brian mopping
            and mowing
with the flannel title
        and the cookie cutter
commerce
  alienating the good dough
of my estate
                forcing alive
the reactionary
                griffin

version of Poland
                tremulous quinces
of the aristocracy
                      shoring up
feudal decay
                cloud audience
of the noble jaw
                  all half-stuffed
with their birth-grapes
                  mulberry juice
and beetroot
                  shot-up and
totally without feeling
                    dreaming
in a time of peace
                the social good of
future far
                a nation without
apocalypse family
                a nation without
democracy
                  in practice

democracy
has always meant
giving money freedom
to move
around the sky
Easyjet galleons
advocates bent over
covert preparations
winter vinegar
celeriac
swede
capons
SPAM
monks in the pantry
going incredibly mad
stewing split peas
flinching
the monastery stalked
by Blinky
Pinky
Inky
and Clyde

a greenish-grey
                    intellectual ghost
and the sun burning
        in a 12th century church
a fridge
                    beach-burning
the dunes full of bombs
                    Bea agonising
over an aerial view
                    of St Louis
Missouri
        Kat playing the drums
with her eyeballs
                    punctiliously
surveying the
        stitch of rocket seeds
or so I thought but
                    who was that
on the grass
                    over a peat fire
singing her lover
                    back from the sea

while I blink

             Brian's latest

off my corneas

             levitating queasily

over a bird skelly

               out there

small and embattled

             tiny white detail

like a foam cusp

    goes the memory ferry

say

            that's Fionnphort

and this is Iona

             I am on Staffa

butchering puffins

    it doesn't matter which

Mendelssohn crowbar

    you cannot move for

rainbows putting their

             feet down

for ships that

            were once there

we've got Easter
                    approaching
we've got dad
     coming down the road
with a pink pram
                   hand aloft
we've got scampi
           and constipation
Aidan east for
               resurrection tennis
with cassock hunks
        of another tonsure
in bruisey England
              rude di clima
dolcissimo di storia
               really a diary
of o yay fountains
          billiard invocations
emerald green
        parkland undesigned
designed
        and envy and despair

and walking along
                the pious paths
of Rochdale cemetery
                        mum
I feel as though
                through this whole
relationship
                I have completely
betrayed
                        myself
that kind of headstone
                sour wind
in the arms of the tree
                frozen in waving
over remembrance
                the book of names
alderman
                        thirty-second
face of his age
                        much-loved
much-manned
                young captain

noia patrizia

                ti è intorno

and of you

                and is you

in fact not ash

                but doily soil

no lovers

                of the pioneers

terse merchants

                burning spite off

chains of Woodbines

                chicken dinner

make us grateful

                facing wasteland

you duff forebears

                who died dreaming

we live dead in

                shapes of limestone

granite lockdown

                Rome and Rochdale

uncle Roy but

                feet from Gramsci

beside the canal

                overhead

like a thought

           a flight of locks

glass aqueduct

              the Irk

in snooker emerald

            slug lucency

beneath the sky lakes

              schiarite

and dreaming now

             of the split

English sky

              it's clear

Cromwell's laughter

            before Naseby

was the biggest

             god-directed

sunbeam ever

             the future

for the time being

             put off

I can tell you

           sirs

what I would not have

       though I cannot

what I would

       the problem

as ever

         the event

we get there

       such a little house

I thought it was so big

        and that is

sad

      we cannot get back

the body

       of the business

empire

       what we'd like's

compulsion

       providence

the spine

      of history

Deeplish
                    Ashfield and
if Heybrook
                    fell asleep in Jesus
wheatsheaf beehive
                    Arrow Mill
all listed buildings
            with the weather over
are storage units
                what they mean
when seen
            and what they store
hot air
                    the cold front
its soft fore
            to Morecambe Bay
Flookburgh
                charter fair day
broke as
                        loo roll
wet fall
                    snowflakes

now is

        Brian crisp

against the dry stone wall

        this wind will

never let you *rest*

        by air

we're inside fire

        sea army

of white crests

        no boats go tilting

constant chimney fluting

        the present

held back

        day after day

like parted waves

        around

the present

        walls detritus

and a glue of water

      birds blown sideways

fistfuls

        snowflakes

after lunch

                compost

raised beds

           smothered thuds

Kat and Bea the

                rhubard

beetroot

                   rocket

kale

              or trying

to make

            sense quickly

in outer space

    nothing can get to you

dusk confusing

       itself with afternoon

morning with night

             I find myself

more and more

            a yeoman

half-conscious

         of agile minnows

of the private sector

                    Dyson

lord of the adjacent

                    ventilator

the entire economy

               a false message

of lethargy

                  the truth is

at this latitude

               the sea becomes

a kind of land

                  not land

but solid state

                the weight

holding you up

              like an anvil

or a tuna steak

              lean muscle

as though you were

          between two walls

small baggage

              of history

one weak root

                    a mung bean

proper croft door

                              Kat

Bea

                          look up

white wall

                    nine woodlice

well when

                Laurence called

with news of his

                new fatherhood

grief

                        terror

the feeling beyond

                  of simply

the baby

        the extra-egotistical

reality of care

            the circumstances

comfort like

                  stuckness

well I walked

        down to the sea

with Kat

        and the thing is

the waves *were* milk

        milk and Kat said

blue trifle

     and really astonishing

glass tubes

      stretching their backs

because also muscle

      and then collapsing

into a wide

        and disturbed

lather of milk

          sometimes

exploding backwards

         one wet duck

fishing at the lips

     not a duck of course

muscly bird

       waterproof

providing

        the cliffs there

really are tall

        cities of birds

this heavy pulse of

        signals from

remote storm

        and we didn't want

a kid any more

        than we had

at breakfast

        at the start of this

I kept ringing

        people up

to check they

        hadn't changed

something creaturely of

        incoming parenthood

like a wide wave

        I do not like

the anonymity

        it brings

the sudden memory
        of virus Barcelona
and bacchic slap
        of ballsack
through the wall
        police café
manchego
        for the local force
the mild vegan
        dipping his
little beard
        in cashew yoghurt
the poignance
        of the last plate
of padron peppers
        for the establishment's
foreseeable future
        its physical
high green
        and astonishing
desertion of
        the midnight streets

now Brian came out
            and cornered me
Kat and Bea
                        asleep
under black rugs
                this is where
it's time
            to have it out
no really
                talk I mean
I've been hanging
            round flirtatiously
for weeks now
                bullion man
just listen here
                mouth full of
Bunny Wailer
                        Hair
it's the age of Aquarius
            take off your nappy
and put on your
                consequences

boars in Barcelona
feel that medieval
centrepoint
lifting from your
seesaw
Brian had
all manner of flora
dangling around
his head
fennel
milkweed
delicate bilberries
in haemorrhoidal clusters
tucked behind
frank green leaves
what did you do
during the war
every breath
shaking the organic
matter like a garden
disco and defensive
fringe

I blissed out

                as nothingness

back then

             now I hold close

to the edge

                Brian you

desirable

                arch-enemy

thought in

                painted face

what vanishes

                through you

and to where

                white fire

Westray

                tatters

tenant

                briefly

of a parcel

                of your

absent hand

                your servant

the hummock
                    with its flat hat
its tributaries
                    of dumb sheep
its high pool
                    of frogspawn
today is
                    escape where
in space
                            in time
relentlessly
                    backwards
my neck is broken
            I am from a horror
what I take for the
                    horizon is
the wrong
                    horizon
today is
            it's behind you
a monumental
                    excursion

Eddie Ratter
        stepping into sunlight
from the workshop
        taking off his mask
to greet us
        flicking through
the vintage cars
        Land Rover
even Bentley
        next to his green
Mustang
        Michael's dad
went mad
        or was it his wife
madness round
        that house
like starlings
        from the hot
tub like the dark
        veil of a table
fan spinning
        over a blaze

thirteen or
        fifteen dropping
children invicible
         as memories
as artificial
           twelve or
fourteen lobster creels
       down into sandy
clearings on the bed
    and the wind got up
thirteen or
        fifteen feet high
and the motor
        dropped off too
that Michael
      he's the world's most
laid-back man
         but Ralph just
his father
        his dead brother
two years old
        and later

are you from
                one of the islands
with this big shop
                not four deep
like the early pioneers
                no Evie
strip of sand
                I walk my dog
just let me
                nothing
nothing
                but the broch
the checkout
                fallen in
isn't any
                any longer
strip of sea
                a lot of lives
fallen in there
                roof of a
strange seeds
                fall uselessly

into strange earth
                    bed just drops
twenty five feet
            and three tides meet
huge spray
                    on the table
I would say
            fifty beetroot seeds
suspended
        the water discoloured
obscure cadets
                    streaks as
vanishing as
                the ranger of
the forest
                of Weybridge
remember
            St George's Hill
don't judge what's
                    underneath
by what's on top
                    false leaves

and over the fence
                                wild
madder
                                lichen
Brian right to the wire
                        blithe cheek
on the cheese string
                        and that little doll
king Esau
                        on a small and
because imaginary
                                "harmless"
hill
 kneecaps going great guns
the effort
                        of waving
snap-waggling
                        the head to roll
balsa wooden
                        barely heavy
down among
                        the espionage grass

the unpeopled field
                    what desert
where the standing stones
    Landlords and Tennants
pesticide-wage
                    the shadows
shaken loose
    who brought the ground
alive
                whose lives rang
in the ground
                yesterday reborn
bereaved
        but limping forth you
great Ones of the Earth
                        a carrot
a parsnip
    in the Parish of Walton
corn
            of amnesiac fortune
righteous labour
        the sweat of our brows

a frozen

        moment but
the moment still

        a hard flower
opening

        did you not see
raised bed

        germinal
my hand

        moon-weight
ghost of a landscape

        with ten thousand
copyholders

        this last year
stretched out

        coaxing the roots
with heavy model

        into the muck
rootless figures

        finding themselves
outside

        you did not see

that green shoot

                a hand

that has not

                gone down

it is stretched out

                still

clutches mine

                fellow creature

evening of Greece

                black paper cut-out

tonight

                the super moon

space lighthouse

                white absolute

looking at it

                just like looking

at anything else

                elsewhere

truth is

                at this latitude

space becomes

                sea

that thing
        holding you up
my hand
        driving several
tides into
        the dissolution
of your chariot
        that flesh
and as the tidal waves
        part
they reveal themselves
        to be parliament
down the aisle
        progressing a king
as a broom
        across
the glass avenue
        240,000 miles
I am every last regent
        of this moment
and every last
        head of my court

is perfect moon
                    the boulevard
like cedars
                    shine on
with the light's full face
                    but the instant
though diamond
                    melts off
a pain
                    I'd disavow
by the wrong image
                    of the future
the present is
                    put beyond
itself
          by the frozen image
of the past
                    the present is
put behind
                    itself
I do not now know
          where the waste is

but come with me
        beginning to Plant
and Manure
             the phone goes
Clive
       white heaps of flour
ash
              soft pozzolan
Kat and Bea pressing
           the soil in
with thumb bamboo
       and get some sand
wash it
         get the salt off it
even if you go round
      with a carrier bag
pick up sheepshit
   whatever muck you see
eight or nine inches down
      you'll get potatoes
a sign of the deep
   forgetfulness of the time

Friday evening
            before I look at
a tin of chickpeas
            as a can of Holsten
Bea has sliced radishes
            very fine in a pickle
ginger
                        soy sauce
mustard seed
            hugely pink
Brian in the fireplace
            trying to remember
The Earle of Salisbury
            over Jacques Brel
gargling Flemish
   zonde liefde warme liefde
and on the horizon
            like a pillow
is a fillet steak
            there's one for me
and one for you
            Shackleton boohoo

two hunks fade
        like rose-pink twilight
on a two-step of cloud
        en route to my mouth
soft cut
                think you can get
away with anything
                if your jumper
is Norwegian enough
                I was a sailor once
and Shackleton
                        was dead
buff brute
                        cardiac barrel
ice floe
                        dick floe
pickaxe surgery
                on the donkey
the donkey death throes
                        so it goes
Cherry-Garrard
                and the widows

of Captain Scott's egos
   I don't care who they are
though
            or what they do
or how
           they all have
the same face
        of duff-cut stone
so Shackleton
         I was walking
through time
       like a Mandalorian
and suddenly
       the ceiling was low
and the lighting lower
   and the ambience oily
and o
                ho
ho
        how I treasure
how I found
       his heart

red heart
          preserved in duck fat
below deck
                on the last tug
bound for Canton
                    red heart
yellow fat
               in a tin can
whose label bore
     the emblem of a toucan
I was far from home
     thinking of Hog Lane
of lying prone
                for seven days
in the abstract
               heaven of smoke
but even so I shed a tear
          for my grandma
still farming Corn Flakes
          in her queer field
beside the Cerne Abbas
               triceratops

Brian was
                pissing himself
you've had the strings
                of my noggin
today Brutus
                not to mention
the massacre
        at the oatcake priory
I moved my hand
                it was among
a hoard of smashed
                oat biscuits
I looked around
        pajamas in disarray
the fog of a stranger's
        dream had blown off
and the sea gone
                fifteen shades
of questing blue
                where were you
and where were you
                and where was I

Birkenhead Iron Works
  innumerable expert hands
a memory in the frame
                        Wales
the Bristol Channel
                        a trace
the bay of St Ives
                   Land's End
a trace
           St Michael's Mount
Yarmouth Roads
                        a trace
the Bay of Biscay
             Cape Finisterre
Madeira
                    Teneriffe
Cape Town
              Delagoa Bay
touching at Ceylon
                  for coals
the Straits of Malacca
                Singapore

from Liverpool
                    Hull
early winter dark
    from Chatham in spring
from Portsmouth in July
                    autumn
whatever
                out of this fleet
dispersed across the water
                    in time
in space
                    comes I
one
        unmistakeable mast
among the naked forest
    of interchangeable masts
I don't say which
                the which is
unimportant
                the waters blue
the weather
                on our side

the sun

                an iron ball

the sun

                a golden ball

the sun

        a sticky, brown ball

the sun

           a barbarian eye

the sun a socket

      for there was no sun

the sun white

        and the sky black

the sun black

        and the sky blackened

                the sun

      swollen to fill the sky

the sun

        swollen to swallow

the earth

        a fleet of warships

the sun

  a hundred and forty suns

the long

        low Nemesis

Christian Sweetpea

 sleeping on the poop deck

the hold full

        of hollow bibles

a portrait of

        Karl Gützlaff

on the piano

        inventions weeping

from atolls

        text floating swollen

in the loaded waters

flyering into one continent

after another

 under the blind telescopes

of the gunboats

        concerned not to

magnify

        but to fire

dead eyeballs

        into the view

the mist

               the mist
the damn mist
    clearing on the bridge
of the Starship Enterprise
              my love
my love
              Afghanistan
operational white man
           poppy-headed
lump of chicken
             blast-hot
from a Rocket Boil
          flavour trick of
the apparent view
     of Cuckmere Haven
ace surf shining
         childish impulse
loving eating
         loving plastic
so beloved
      here eat plastic

and these bombers
    are like droplets of lead
undetectable
           remember
that one mast
        among the fleet
fiddling Spithead
         Plymouth
is coming to kill you
         fol-de-rol
without understanding
  without even disturbance
of the love of its mother
  marmalade in the Congo
I eat whatever I like
           sirrah
to express my liking
      we had known this
inconstant sun
        from our cradles
the firmament of words
      makes killing easy

Odessa my arse
        there in Delagoa Bay
a matchstick armada
        the "wooden walls"
of England
        chuffily giving up
its woodpiles
                to the iron gut
of warranted purpose
  wherefore especial thanks
to Captains Tiepin
                        Catnip
and Batshit
                        incidentally
barbarians
                        no
these are the curtains
    I wear around my head
say
                        full sail
a mental picture
        of Shahrazad

the first

                second

third

                fourth

(fifth)

                (sixth)

(seventh)

                (eighth)

(ninth)

             how many

children

       the new Jerusalem

anyway

       same as the old boss

a new heaven

          and a new earth

for I was an obedient

            undergraduate

with a prominent

          adam's apple and

God shall wipe away

           all the tears

light trembling in glass
                Sunday morning
bleeding out
                of fresh-cut grass
and there shall be
                no more death
a pinkness fallen on
                the adam's apple
neither sorrow
                nor crying
a freshly-shaven
                chicken face
neither shall there be
                any more pain
the note rises
                a bolt
into bi-plane Valhalla
                and widens flat out
like lightspeed
                a wingspan
for the former things
                are passed away

Miles
                dismissed
in the salmon-pink chinos
      of the helpless aristo
vanishes
            for the last time
Abba
                Father
beyond the rood screen
      whereat the gin sea
for the bums
           of the civilised
are but fallen faces
  how they sit abandoned
and speaking incoherently
     into their chino-seats
from the walls of heaven
      turned to emerald
porphyry
              jade
jade
              jade

cataracts
        split the dismal deck
this hallucination
        of ice-fresh water
from the fields of sleep
        the almighty
weather fronts
        green bruises
purple streaks
    falling over themselves
in bulk
        making sprats
of whales
        the swell under
summoning
        tyl
on a hyl
        banked up
on cloud enormous
        the lapidary pile
as devyses hit
        the apostel John

that military city
                    bristling with
amphetamine-rapid
            absolutely alert but
utterly shit-stupid
                            guns
and rich
            with rigor mortis
every stiff layer
                    of overkill
jasper
                        saffer
calsydoyne
                    emerade
sardonyse
                        rybé
crysolyt
                        beryl
topayse
                    crysopase
jacyngh
                    amatyst

its streets all gold
          its river wide open
its whole
          enormous gemstone
instaneity
          out of the firmament
of waters
                    like a war
memorial made
          of arrested song
this was the kind of shit
          we saw in the sky
cruising on
                    the ocean blue
to blow our holy dope
     our round brown cargo
our soft and hard
          expansive weapon
of extraction
                    deep into
the interior
                    of China

where the silver
               gathers itself
like woodlice
               into jackpots
at the bedsides
               of the economy
its whacked addicts
               where six Jesuits
wander quantum
               in the unsolved zone
where Thomas Manning's
               tears become his beard
his beard his tears
               to be his tears
in an eternal loop
               at seeing Lhasa
and where Qianlong
               questions the existence
of an English
               high chair
heaven does not
               have two suns

so it was
                with deep relief
I made the ferry
    from the Faroe Islands
idle at Scrabster
              a grandparent
the green trawler
              dip its orange
hopes into the swell
 the Stonehenge delegation
take a punt
        from Rackwick Bay
and Mark's boat throw
          its red sails open
down the long
              marine lane
of the past
        as Brian released
his face from my brain
            coming over
the last rise
              onto

St Columba's Bay
                   some graceful
chimera disembarking
                   its lucky coracle
imagine your brain
                   in a mask
I could see again
              Kat was chopping
coriander
              a form of gas
that turns into clouds of
              Daniel Craig
and drifts murderously
              across Macao
oof
              small black bird
with the white headband
              back on the grass
all tombs calm
              there were events
that had not been
                   attended to

Easter Sunday
             a heavy day
for the oven
             twenty carbonised
hot cross buns
             their crosses
faintly showing
             Bea in a headscarf
freshening the quarters
             conversation of ash
incense
             small goblet of water
the black circle
             of the infernal diver's
vacant face
             Jonny Cash
Kat reading
             Diane di Prima
what are these
             I let go of
many things
             I am not ready

to let go

                one by one

the clear sky

                   fills with

small lights

                of its divers

stars

          firmament of waters

that infinite shipment

                of dissipating

impulses

                   glorified

good wishes

               floating candles

those silhouettes

            who walked off

soundlessly

                  forever

the grief goes on

                     real

extensive

                hollow

as the opening
   under the loaded ground
Michael's torch
      swinging of the barn
mouth down below
        Noup Head usual
a pattern of satellites
   low houses in the land
and sea one block the only
       shtum of red
brake lights
        another island
Venus absolutely high
      and white acute
and seven in the morning
       comes again
the same
         assassin
Lightborn
     to comfort you
and bring you
      joyful news

I east myself
                    into the west
I hold the pose
                beginning to find
scale most
                        relative
like Gulliver
                    like Alice
whom I prefer
                    is the warrior
in fact
            a suspension bridge
because then
                    Nick enters
on the milk white steed
        back of the outlandish
silverfish
                    all dressed in
Lincoln green I mean
                    whistle-ribbons
floating harmonium
                        and then

today's fiend
        Richard Branson
that grimace
          forces entry
walking on stilts
        of infinitely long
and thin
         coin columns
spring robot legs
          as it were
hovercraft
         tottering atop
the Necker Island
    Croydon reacharound
and in fact Nick
       Gloriana-faced
disguising a guitar
          as a lute
for John Barleycorn
     was England's tonsil
on a superyacht
         chest-fretting

among the looser

                  acute speeds

of rum and cocaine that

    troubling circular blade

the periphery

            the west of his days

when Richard

                came waving

in the confusion of spray

              and imaginary

you are naïve

                  to imagine it

spectral net

                commonwealth

strangled leatherbacks

           disposed shammies

strops on

    petrochemical compost

that more and more

            diminishing vista

caved heads of eggs

           garlanded with yolk

who knows what
                    quantities of
miasmatic
                    imagination
puff themselves
                    away to ever
smaller islands
          centres of themselves
fringes
          of the imagination
afraid
                         fringes
of the imagination
                    assured
fringes
          of the imagination
secured
     and we know with what
razor wire
               of a certain sleeve
perhaps of
                    grey

metal

                        grey water
I am not running
        the expanse is present
at once
                        I am alone
locked in the position
  of an unearthed fragment
one after another
                as the museum
barely knows its shame
                with its guileful
self-accusing
                        chorus
that which we are
                        we are
emptied out
                into the sameness
of our staying
                        put
accidental but
                        just so

that is the function
                of *this* island
enclosure
                of the instant
instant of a
                fever-dream
of an inventory
                secluded as a
substrate
                hurtling there
with mum
                with dad
I wake each morning
                reborn as a land
sorry
                a *lamb*
my voiceless legs
    shafts of pure presence
going down
                into nothing
proof of my
                innocence

how can one
        come round again
so quickly
        sweat with Jillian
if you wanna buy jeans
        think about that
then lunch again
        so quickly
this is getting to be
        a habit
Bea stretching
        Kat having a shower
a number of woodlice
        dead in the pan
since yesterday
        the sea
quite still
        blue actually
lead carried off
        by the wind
some lumps of ash
        caught in the grass

Brian blowing around
            outside the window
on the back of
            the black bird
with its white headband
      clearly having a blast
muttering something
            hard to catch
between the buffets
            of the breeze
muttering
            and laughing
I can't quite
            believe what
I am hearing
            I *will* not
believe what
            I am hearing
are you a hobbit
            or a Hobbist
are you a hobbit
            or a Hobbist

jellyfish head

                  I

joyne not

           myself

to any settled

           congregation

I shit

           myself

in a fen and

           splintered by

Victoriana-barley-bent

           William Perkins

leaning over the wind

  of Stourbridge Common

breathing fields of masters

           rackrent destitutes

wicker fires from

           pondscum sockets

splintered by

           time

times

           and dividing of time

splintered by

                Archy

the king's fool

                  who

by his office

           splintered by

the pepper of the EIC

   divided into many heads

splintered by

            the same parish

and in the same manner

           splintered by

Prince Maurice

         with a small army

splintered by

        their mind set afloat

in the wide sea

           of monopolies

splintered by the psalm

    my lung and forehead

prospect of

         that crown of glory

by
                Queen Elizabeth
of famous memory
                            by
the voice of fear is
                if I had done this
and by
        Penn in the Caribbean
Goodson in the Baltic
                    and by vogues
for paper constitutions
            schism and sauciness
and by unfixed
                    variable rents
and by the boom in Alfred
        who am universal love
and by power
                        not right
I come to market
                desperate with
remorseless logic
    disguised as legs of lamb

and wake as
                    sunrise
always the day after
                    new white
archipelago
  of shit across the window
the sea out far
                    fulmars
above all
                    wading
dinosaurs
            the time before
in their own element
                abstract mum
white specks
                and dad
the tractor beam
        and more than foam
and let themselves
                fall heavily
precisely
            into splashes

when

        who's that

rattle in the hallway

        just shot out

gelatine transparency

        corner of the eye

onto the track

     up the green brackets

had enough has it

      damn poltergeist

jellied pork

        of the pie

of my own crust

      past the lambs

prosthetic innocents

     split-pinning around

past the hens

       ding dong

ding dong

       past the long

extension through

     days they call cows

that's no joke
                    how thick
a metal ring is
                    Old MacDonald
through its nose
                    never forget
at the Dounby show
                    the red and blue
machinery
                    there he goes
shine and flash
                    of a sud
Kat and Bea
          come look ribboning
with the tarmac's
                    grey line
and then up
                    the track up
the hummock
                    with is flat hat
trimmed wick
                    available neck

for the head
        dissolved like a flock
of starlings like salt
        in a boiling pot
when the blade
        passed through
John Brown's
        experimental
wind turbine
        wood spar
spruce rib
        blades
chugging like
        a stuck Spitfire
obviously Brian
        being all head
I think
        that's when
not before
        it wasn't
premeditated
        he thought up

an aside
  while you finish your pint
about The Dam Busters
                in this film
a group of mods
          set off on scooters
to the Ruhr
                to punch
a couple of dams
                to bits
and drown
              a thousand
actually it's mods
  they end up drowning
accidentally
           about the film
Quadrophenia
         where nineteen
sentimental racist
      Lancaster bombers
fly into Maderia Terrace
  and blow it the fuck up

the bomb
           monsoon in Basildon
Teddington experimental
                     ship tank
o gravelly
                     unh
granola complex
           good morning Sussex
today
                     snakes wipe
the corn sides
           I pen another episode
of Anthony Horowitz's
                most Cluedo
dork leather
                red rubber face
my child
                     Jacob
plays welly
           in the pond margin
with a squelchy sprout
                from the town

sudden distillation
                    of flab
contraction in
        the new conservatory
suck crystals
                    calcium oxalate
in darkness
                    into definition
at sunset
        with the warm beef
brayne panne
                    Oxshott
and the ribbons
        on the maypole
are South Western
                    Southern
Great Western
        and Greater Anglia
traaaaaaaaaynes
        and the stake is
Ruhr steel
                    I think

that's when

                    not before

he resolved

              to test the bomb

from the hilltop

                    Brian did

the head

              the head of state

great power

                  over nothing

projected stack

                 of sandstone

beautiful and sheer

                and sumer is

the Wellington

              comes overhead

put out your ears

          and sumer is icumen

diuretic frequency that

        small intestine hooker

loved of

             hamshanks on hikes

rumbles in the sun
　　what pink exquisiteness
the sea stacks tower
　　　　　　　and applaud
the orcas stitch
　　　the spangling surface
of the water
　　　　diaphanous droplets
tip-tremble a
　　　platoon of sharp stalks
dolphin agitation
　　　　rolling sweet diesel
and the bomb door
　　　　　of the Lancaster
it slowly dawns
　　　　　　and the bomb
rolls out
　　　　Kat and Bea and I
aghast below
　　　　　　expecting
that iron ball
　　　　　but no

it is
        King Arthur's head
embalmed in
            Berlusconi oil
and sumer is
        how stoical he looks
though dead
    and sumer is icumen in
decapitated
            groweþ sed
and bloweþ med
           his deadness
makes his look
    and springþ þe wde nu
persisting
            sing cuccu
the silenced sky and
    black a poisoned bolus
nonsense
        how it plummets
how the azure main
      receives it carelessly

and Brian finally
          begins to shred up
like the aurora
          and a stillness come
the hillside down
                    listen how
awe bleteþ after lomb
          lhouþ after calue cu
bulluc sterteþ
                    bucke uerteþ
murie sing cuccu
   the sun coming like it is
cuccu cuccu
                    when it is
the end of the
                    what it is
wel singes þu cuccu
                    so hard
ne swik þu nauer nu
   for now only sometimes
sing cuccu nu
                    sing cuccu

23 March – 1 May 2020

Acknowledgements

Love and thanks to Kat and Bea, with whom I shared the strange time documented in this poem. Love and thanks to Verity, at whose behest I initially wrote it. Love and thanks to Will, Hugh, Bella, my dad, my mum and Aug who all read it. Love and thanks to Dante, Gam, Matt and Dave for recording it with me, and to Kashif for putting the recording of it out. Love and thanks to Azad for bigging it up. Love and thanks to James Byrne for his incisive and supportive editorial comments on it. Love and thanks to Aaron Kent for publishing it.

LAY OUT YOUR UNREST